THE BIG BOOK OF CZECH REPUBLIC

AN EDUCATIONAL COUNTRY TRAVEL PICTURE BOOK FOR KIDS ABOUT HISTORY, DESTINATION PLACES, ANIMALS AND MANY MORE

Copyright @2023 James K. Mahi

All rights reserved

The Czech Republic is a country in Europe.

Official short name	Czechia
National symbol	double-tailed lion
Religion	Roman Catholic (10.6%) Orthodox (3%) Protestant (includes Czech Brethren and Hussite) 1.1% Atheist (39.8%) Non or Undeclared (79,4%)
 Czech Republic – independence Day	1 January 1993

National bird: The black stork is considered the national bird of the Czech Republic. It is a large, black bird with a long neck and legs.

National tree: The oak tree is considered the national tree of the Czech Republic. It is a symbol of strength and endurance.

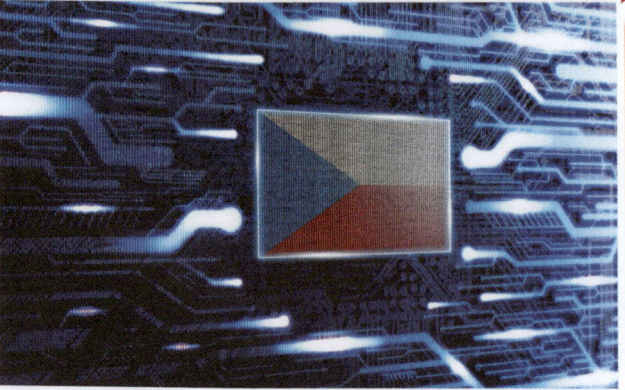

Official name: The official name of the Czech Republic is the Czechia.

People: The people of the Czech Republic are called Czechs.

Size: The Czech Republic is about the size of the state of Pennsylvania. It has a total area of 78,866 square kilometers.

Largest city: The largest city in the Czech Republic is Prague. It has a population of over 1.2 million people.

Population: The population of the Czech Republic is about 10.7 million people.

Overpopulation: The Czech Republic is not considered to be overly populated. The population density is about 137 people per square kilometer.

World's land: The Czech Republic occupies about 0.07% of the world's land.

Time zones: The Czech Republic is in the Central European Time (CET) zone.

Nickname: The Czech Republic is sometimes nicknamed "the Land of a Thousand Spires" because of its many Gothic and Baroque churches and cathedrals.

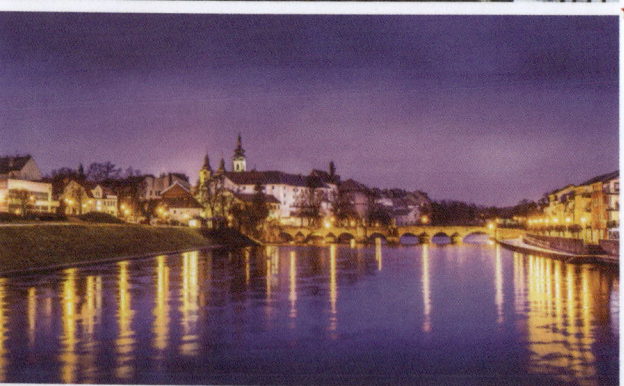

First rulers: The first rulers of the Czech Republic were the Přemyslid dynasty. They ruled the country from the 9th century until the 14th century

The capital city is Prague, known as the "City of a Hundred Spires."

Prague Castle is one of the largest castles in the world.

The Czech Republic used to be a part of Czechoslovakia.

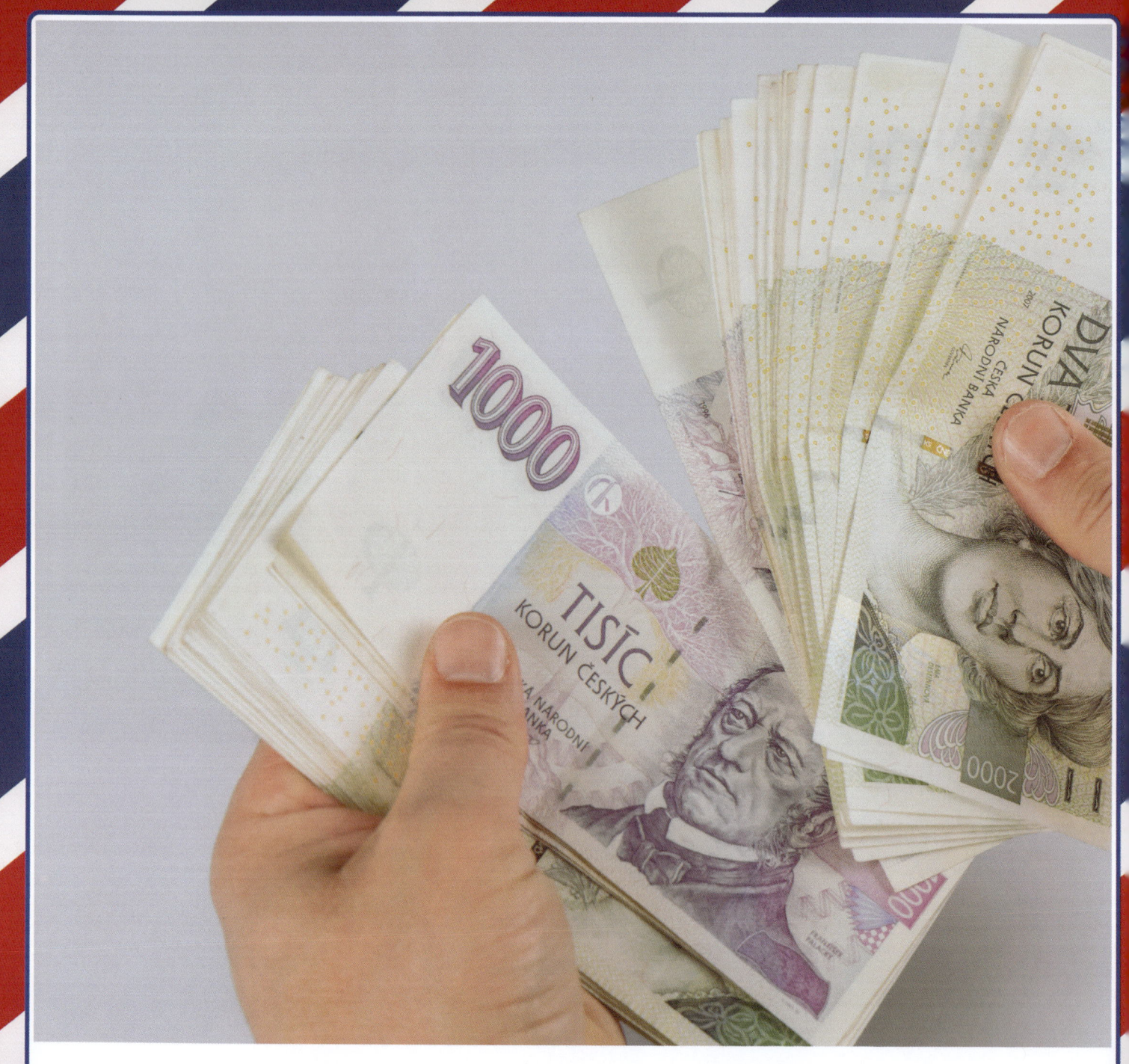

The currency is called the Czech koruna.

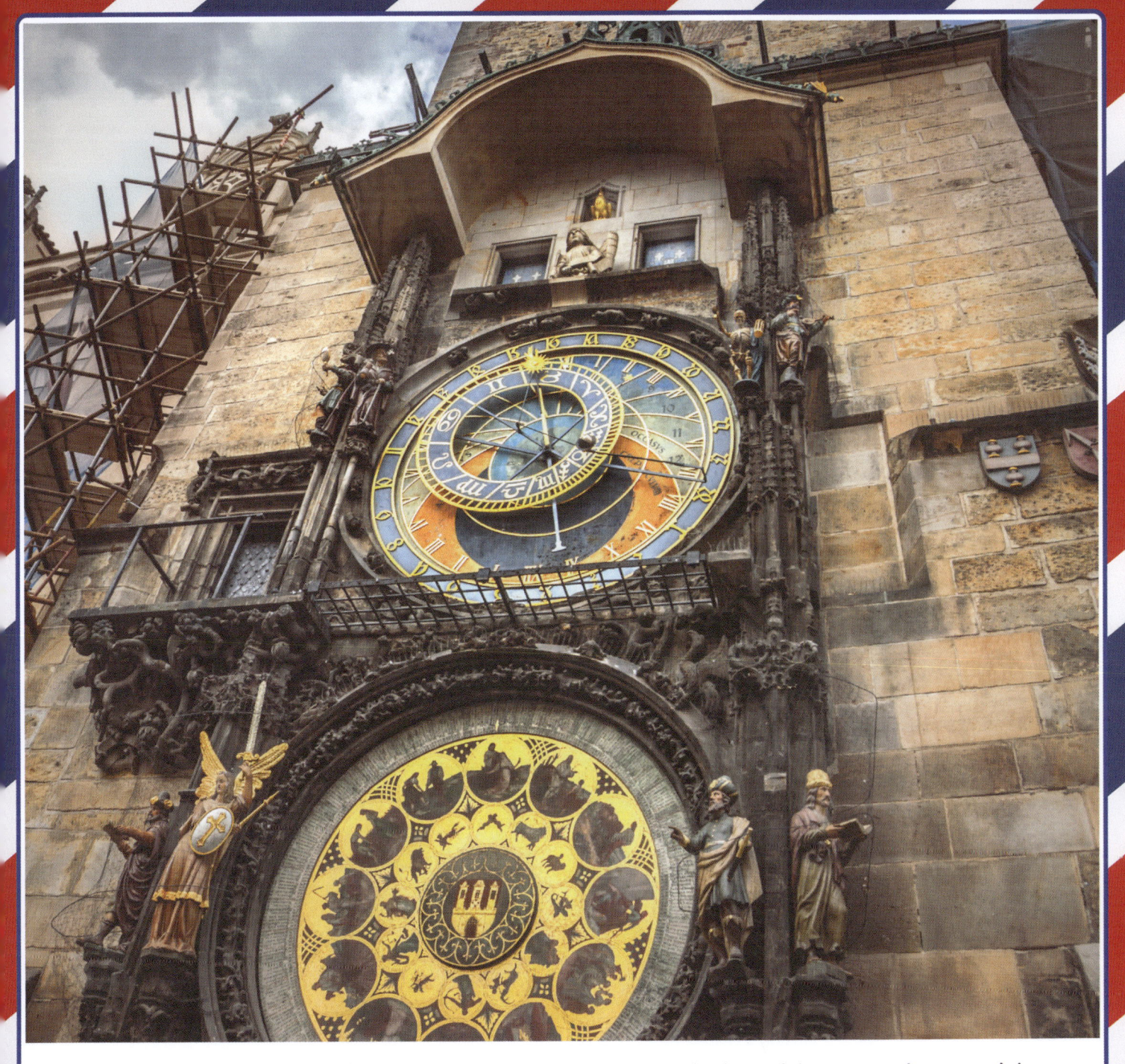

The Astronomical Clock in Prague is one of the oldest in the world.

The Charles Bridge is a historic bridge with statues of saints.

The national sport is ice hockey.

The traditional music includes the accordion and the violin.

Czechia, Bohemia, and Moravia are historical regions within the country.

The Vltava River flows through Prague.

The country has many hot springs and spas.

The famous author Franz Kafka was born in Prague.

There are many puppet theaters in the country.

The Pravčická Gate is the largest natural sandstone arch in Europe.

The town of Český Krumlov has a castle and winding streets.

Czechia has a mix of mountains, forests, and valleys.

The traditional food includes goulash and dumplings.

The Czech Republic has many underground caves to explore.

The town of Kutná Hora has a church decorated with human bones.

The country is famous for its Christmas markets.

The Wallenstein Palace in Prague is known for its beautiful gardens.

The Czech countryside is dotted with picturesque villages.

The folk architecture in some villages is very colorful and unique.

The town of Telč has a square with colorful Renaissance houses.

The Czech Republic is famous for its crystal glassware.

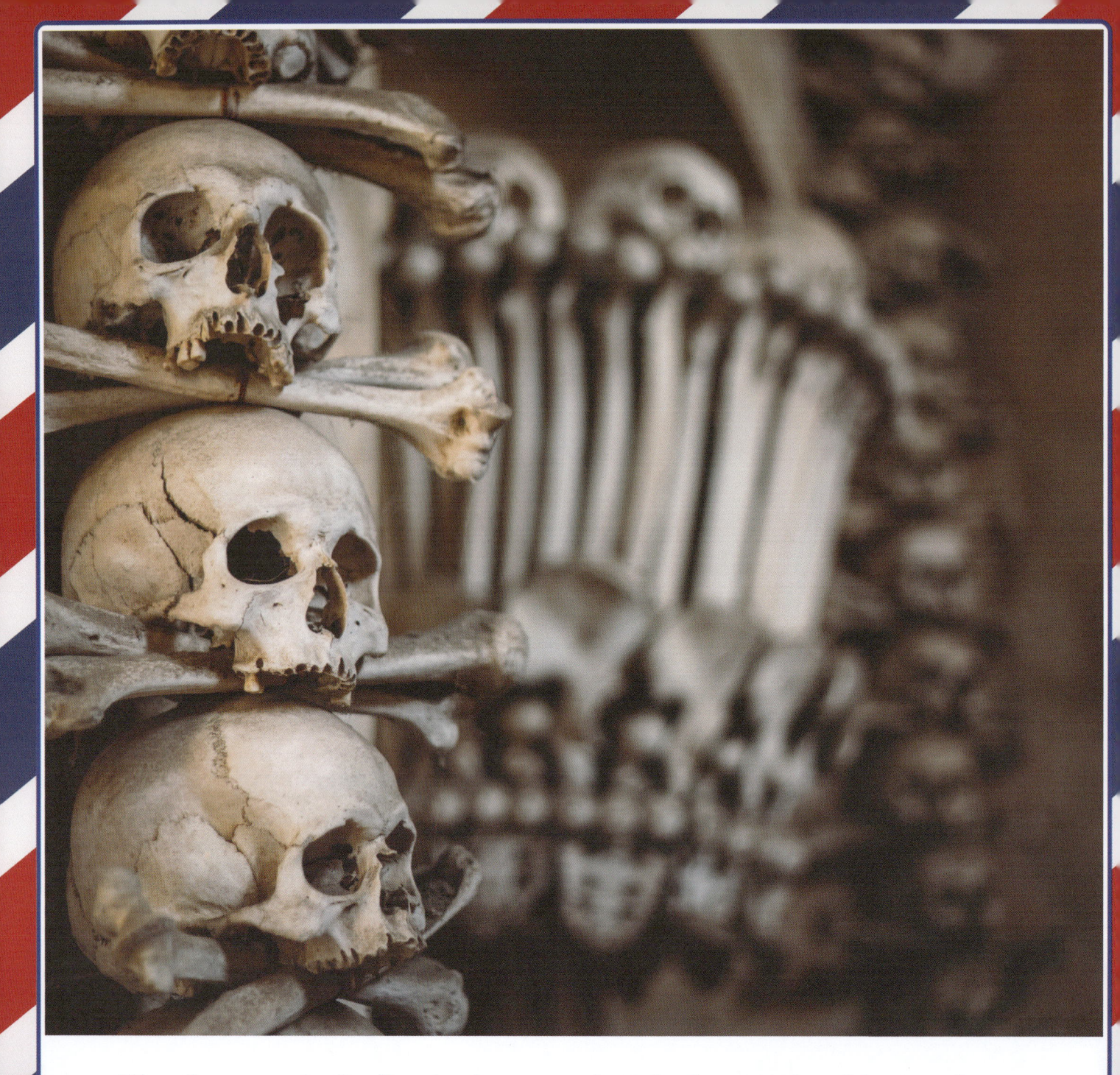

The Ossuary in Sedlec is decorated with thousands of human bones.

Czech people celebrate the Feast of Three Kings on January 6th.

The Krkonoše Mountains are great for skiing and hiking.

The country has a tradition of making delicious gingerbread cookies.

The official language is Czech.

The flag has two colors: white, red, and blue

The country is famous for its delicious pastries called "trdelník."

The Czech Republic is known for making beautiful glass and crystal products.

The country has lots of beautiful castles and chateaus.

The composer Antonín Dvořák was from the Czech Republic.

Pilsner beer was first brewed in the city of Pilsen.

The word "robot" was first used by a Czech writer.

The country celebrates St. Nicholas Day on December 5th.

Czech people celebrate Easter with decorated Easter eggs.

The tradition of making marionettes is very old in the Czech Republic.

The Škoda auto company is from the Czech Republic.

The tradition of spa treatments dates back many centuries.

The Moravian Karst region has stunning limestone formations.

The Villa Tugendhat is an example of modern architecture.

The town of Karlovy Vary is famous for its thermal springs.

TOP 15 TRAVEL TIPS FOR VISITING THE CZECH REPUBLIC

1. Currency and Money: The currency in the Czech Republic is called the Czech koruna (CZK). Make sure to have some local money for small purchases.
2. Public Transportation: Trains, trams, and buses are common for getting around. You can buy tickets at stations or in advance.
3. Language: The main language is Czech, but in tourist areas, English is often spoken. It's helpful to learn a few basic Czech phrases like "hello" (ahoj) and "thank you" (děkuji).
4. Tipping: It's polite to leave a small tip, usually around 10% of the bill, in restaurants and for good service.
5. Important telephone numbers : Police 158, Fire Brigade 150, Ambulance 155
6. Czech Cuisine: Try traditional dishes like goulash, dumplings, and trdelník (a sweet pastry). The beer is famous, too!
7. Cultural Etiquette: Greet people with a smile and a handshake. It's common to wait for the host to say "dobrou chuť" (enjoy your meal) before starting to eat.
8. Opening Hours: Shops and museums might close earlier on weekends and public holidays. Plan your visits accordingly.
9. Czech Castles: The country is known for its stunning castles. Don't miss Prague Castle, Karlštejn Castle, and Český Krumlov Castle.
10. Tourist Cards: Consider getting a Prague Card or other city cards for discounts on attractions and public transportation.
11. Photography: Respect signs that indicate where photography is not allowed, especially in churches and museums.
12. Adapters: The standard voltage is 230V and the outlets are of the European type. Bring an adapter if needed.
13. Czech Festivals: Check if there are any local festivals or events happening during your visit. They're a great way to experience Czech culture.
14. Respect Local Customs: When visiting churches, remove your hat and stay quiet as a sign of respect.
15. Travel Insurance: It's a good idea to have travel insurance that covers medical expenses and unexpected events.

Printed in Great Britain
by Amazon